THE Barbie COOKBOOK

EDDA USA

The Barbie Cookbook

Please be advised that adult supervision is required
for several of the recipes.

Recipes: Unnur Gudrun Palsdottir, Margret Bjarnadottir
Intro stories: Judy Katschke
Photography: Gassi Olafsson
Layout and cover design: Olafur Gunnar Gudlaugsson
Printed in Canada

Distributed by Macmillan

ISBN: 978-1-94078-748-0

www.eddausa.com

Hi, everyone!

Welcome to my cookbook, filled with scrumptious, delicious and mouthwatering recipes for you and your friends.

I love to cook and bake and have even had the idea of opening up my very own restaurant someday. I have a lot of recipes up my sleeve, but the ones in this book are my absolute favorites, the crème de la crème as they say.

The recipes vary in difficulty and complexity, but they all have one thing in common: they taste better when enjoyed with a friend!

So dive in, get cooking and enjoy my favorite recipes.

Barbie

PS: Remember, always have an adult with you in the kitchen!

Getting Started

Keeping it Clean

The number one rule when preparing food in the kitchen is cleanliness. Wear an apron to keep your clothes clean and if you have long hair, tie it up in a ponytail. And before you begin, always wash your hands thoroughly.

Safety First

Sharp knives should never be used without adult supervision. The same goes for the oven and all electrical devices.

It's important to always be extremely careful around knives, scissors, stoves, and ovens. Always ask an adult for permission before cooking.

Reading the Recipe

After having made sure everything is clean and safe, the next order of business is reading through the recipe.

It may be tempting to start dicing and slicing as soon as you read the first word, but you should wait until you have read the whole recipe. There might be an important piece of information at the bottom of the page that you need to know about.

Another reason to read the recipe through to the end is to make sure everything is ready before you start. Gather all the ingredients, as well as all the tools you need to use.

Washing the Produce

The last step in the preparation is to clean the produce. Gather any fruits and vegetables you're using in a colander and rinse well under lukewarm water. Root vegetables should be scrubbed lightly with a brush and water.

Have fun!

List of Contents

Breakfast

Overnight Oatmeal

With berries and nuts

Who says oatmeal has to be lumpy and boring? Not Barbie. She powers up her morning bowl with hearty nuts, juicy berries and a splash of milk.

 ## Ingredients

- 1 cup rolled oats
- 2½ cups whole milk (almond milk for a non-dairy option)
- ½ cup mixed berries
- ¼ cup chopped pecan nuts or any other nut*
- ¼ teaspoon sea salt

 ## Instructions

1) Combine the rolled oats, nuts and sea salt in a bowl and pour the milk over the ingredients.

2) Let the dry ingredients soak in the milk for at least 30 minutes in the refrigerator. You could also let it soak overnight and have it ready in the fridge when you wake up the next morning.

3) Top with mixed berries and serve.

This recipe is great to make with any fruits or nuts you have available! Use what you find in your kitchen cabinets!

Tasty Teddy Bear Bread

With homemade peanut butter

When Barbie, Skipper, and Stacie surprised Chelsea with a Teddy Bear picnic, there was a lot more than teddy bears involved. Packed in their picnic basket were peanut butter sandwiches made extra tasty with berries, bananas, chocolate, and honey!

 Ingredients

This recipe requires adult supervision!

The peanut butter
- 2 cups roasted peanuts
- 1 tablespoon honey
- ½ teaspoon sea salt
- ½–1 tablespoon extra virgin olive oil

Macadamia-chocolate butter
- 2 cups macadamia nuts
- 1 tablespoon honey
- 2 tablespoons cocoa powder
- ½ teaspoon sea salt
- ½–1 tablespoon extra virgin olive oil

 Instructions

The peanut butter
1) Put the peanuts in a blender or food processor, turn it on and watch the peanuts turn into a crumble and then smooth butter.

2) Stop and scrape the sides every 1 or 2 minutes with a spatula to make sure everything blends evenly. Always make sure to turn the blender or food processor completely off before opening it.

3) Add the honey and salt and blend.

4) Add the oil slowly, until the consistency of the peanut butter is thin enough so that you can spread it on bread.

5) Spread on bread, decorate with bananas and blueberries and enjoy!

Macadamia-chocolate butter
1) Put the macadamias in a blender or food processor, turn it on and watch the nuts turn into a crumble and then smooth butter.

2) Stop and scrape the sides every 1 or 2 minutes with a spatula to make sure everything blends evenly. Always make sure to turn the food processor completely off before opening it.

3) Add the honey, cocoa and salt and blend.

4) Add the oil slowly, until the consistency of the macadamia-chocolate butter is thin enough so that you can spread it on bread.

5) Spread on bread, decorate with bananas and blueberries and enjoy!

Strawberry Yogurt Gala

With homemade granola

Fashion-forward Nikki knows how to accessorize. But her creativity doesn't stop there. Give Nikki some plain Greek yogurt and she goes bananas with fruits, crunchy seeds, and mouth watering graham crackers.

This recipe requires adult supervision!

Ingredients

- 1 cup sliced fresh strawberries
- 1½ cup Greek yogurt
- ½ cup whole milk
- 1 cup rolled oats
- 1 tablespoon sunflower seeds
- 1 tablespoon pumpkin seeds
- 2 tablespoons cocoa powder

- ½ teaspoon cinnamon
- 3 tablespoons pure maple syrup
- 2 tablespoons dried blueberries or raisins
- ½ cup dried coconut flakes

Instructions

1) Preheat the oven to 300°F.

2) Use a blender to mix together the fresh strawberries, Greek yogurt and whole milk and set it aside. If a blender is not available, you can use a knife to finely chop the strawberries and mix them together with the yogurt and milk with a spatula.

3) Combine the oats, seeds, cocoa powder, and cinnamon in a bowl.

4) Add maple syrup to the oat combination and mix well.

5) Spread the oat and syrup mixture on a baking sheet and bake in the oven for 10-12 minutes, stirring occasionally.

6) Remove from the oven, add the dried blueberries or raisins, and mix well.

7) Fill a short glass with the strawberry yogurt and top it off with the granola.

8) Alternatively, find a tall glass and put 1–2 tablespoons of the granola in the bottom of the glass. Add the strawberry yogurt on top until the glass is half full. Put half of the coconut flakes on top of the yogurt and fill the glass to the rim with the rest of the yogurt. Top off the glass with a tablespoon of the granola and the rest of the coconut flakes.

Omelet Muffins

Friends are coming for brunch. Should Barbie serve her favorite pepper-packed omelet or bake an easy batch of muffins? With an omelet pan in one hand and a muffin tin in the other, Barbie gets the most *egg-cellent* idea. Omelet muffins!

 Ingredients

- 2¾ cups whole wheat flour
- 2 teaspoons baking soda
- 1 teaspoon ground red pepper
- 1 teaspoon sea salt
- ¾ cups whole milk
- ½ cup vegetable oil
- 2 eggs
- ½ cup diced red pepper
- ¾ cups feta cheese
- 1 cup chopped spinach

Instructions

1) Preheat oven to 375°F.

2) In a bowl, mix the flour, baking soda, ground red pepper, and sea salt.

3) In a different, slightly smaller bowl, mix together the whole milk, vegetable oil, and eggs.

4) Stir the egg mixture into the flour mixture. Then add the diced red pepper, feta cheese, and spinach.

5) Spoon into a muffin pan and bake for 25-28 minutes or until golden brown on top.

Colorful Eggs Sunny Side Up

Barbie's sister Skipper likes to add sunshine to her morning with a new playlist. No wonder she likes her eggs sunny side up. And everyone likes Skipper's favorite recipe, which is as easy as one, two, three; three eggs and three colorful peppers!

 Ingredients

- 1 red pepper
- 1 yellow pepper
- 1 green pepper
- 2 tablespoons olive oil or butter
- 3 eggs
- Pinch of sea salt
- Pinch of white pepper

Instructions

1) Cut the red, yellow, and green peppers to make three rounded slices.

2) Place a pan on the stove and heat 2 tablespoons of olive oil or butter.

3) Put one slice of each pepper on the pan.

4) Crack an egg into each pepper ring, using the pepper as a cooking form. Fry the eggs for 3-5 minutes or until the tops of the whites are set but the yolk is still runny.

5) Season with sea salt and pepper to taste and enjoy.

Homemade Granola

Apple-cinnamon granola with milk

Chelsea lost another tooth but it won't keep her from crunching on Barbie's scrumptious granola – made from rolled oats, fruits and nuts. To Chelsea, Barbie's breakfast granola is delish – and the next best thing to dancing!

This recipe requires adult supervision!

 ## Ingredients

- ½ cup almonds
- ½ cup walnuts
- ½ cup pumpkin seeds
- ¼ cup sunflower seeds
- 1 cup rolled oats
- ½ cup dried cranberries
- ½ cup dates

- 2 tablespoons peanut butter
- ¼ cup maple syrup or honey
- 1 teaspoon vanilla
- 1 teaspoon cinnamon
- 1 teaspoon sea salt
- 1 green apple
- 3 strawberries

 ## Instructions

1) Put the nuts and seeds in a bowl and cover them completely with water. Let them soak for at least 1 hour or overnight.

2) Preheat the oven to 400°F.

3) Drain the nuts and seeds and chop coarsely.

4) Combine the chopped nuts and seeds, oats and cranberries in a mixing bowl.

5) Make a paste out of the dates, peanut butter, maple syrup, vanilla, cinnamon and sea salt by combining these ingredients in a blender or food processor.*

6) Add the date paste to the nut and seed mixture and mix well.

7) Spread the mixture on a baking sheet and bake for about 15 minutes. Stir occasionally.

8) Remove from the oven and let the granola cool for a while.**

9) Chop the apple and strawberries into bite size pieces and serve with the granola and milk.

* If you prefer not to use a food processor you can mix everything together except for the dates. You would then chop up the dates finely and set them aside.

** If you did not use a food processor in step 4, you would then sprinkle the dates over the granola and mix it all together.

Tex-Mex Biscuits

Tex-Mex is one of Skipper's favorite foods. So when it's breakfast time, she gives the cheese a twist with a batch of Tex-Mex biscuits to share with her sisters. It's a tasty way to spice up their morning!

 ## Ingredients

Makes about 12 muffins

- 2 cups all-purpose flour
- ½ cup whole wheat flour
- 1 teaspoon baking powder
- 1 teaspoon baking soda
- 1 carrot
- ½ red pepper
- 1 handful of chopped fresh cilantro
- 1 cup grated cheddar cheese
- ½ cup tomato salsa
- ½ cup corn
- 2 eggs
- ⅔ cup vegetable oil

Instructions

1) Preheat the oven to 350°F.

2) Combine the all-purpose flour, whole wheat flour, baking powder, and baking soda in a bowl.

3) Peel and grate the carrot and chop the red pepper and cilantro into small pieces.

4) Add the grated cheese, salsa, corn, carrot, red pepper and cilantro to the flour mixture and blend.

5) In a separate bowl, whisk together the eggs and vegetable oil. Fold the whisked eggs and oil into the combined cheese and vegetables.

6) Spoon into a muffin tin, bake for 25-30 minutes and enjoy!

Snacks

Sunflower Bread

On sunny days you can always find Barbie outdoors. But when the rain pours, Barbie gets busy baking a warm, sweet, crunchy loaf of her Sunflower Bread. What a quick and savory way to bring sunshine to your day, rain or shine!

Ingredients

- 3 cups whole wheat flour
- 1 cup sunflower seeds*
- 1 cup flax or hemp seeds*
- ½ cup pumpkin seeds*
- ½ cup raisins or dried cranberries
- 3 teaspoons baking powder
- 1 teaspoon sea salt

- 2½ cups plain yogurt
- 1 cup milk

* Alternatively, you can pick one of these seeds. Don't forget to increase the amount, though!

Instructions

1) Preheat the oven to 400°F.

2) Mix all the dry ingredients together in a bowl.

3) Stir together the yogurt and milk and mix with the dry ingredients.

4) Pour the mixture in a bread pan and bake for 50–60 minutes or until the top of the bread has turned a slightly darker brown.

5) Take the bread out of the oven and remove from the bread pan.

6) Best served slightly warm with a lot of butter!

Apple & Pomegranate Salad

With pecan and walnut oil

An apple a day may keep the doc away but Barbie's Apple and Pomegranate Salad keeps everyone coming back for more. Lucky for Barbie, she has a bowl big enough for this minty, crunchy, nutty salad.

 Ingredients

Salad
- 1 green apple
- ¼ red onion
- Handful fresh cilantro
- Handful fresh mint leaves
- 1 pomegranate

Dressing
- ¾ cups extra virgin olive oil
- ¼ cup balsamic vinegar
- ½ teaspoon sea salt
- ½ teaspoon pepper

Instructions

1) Chop the green apple into small pieces.

2) Finely chop the cilantro and the mint leaves, after removing them from their stems.

3) Cut the onion into thin slices and each slice into tiny bites.

4) Cut the pomegranate in two and remove the seeds.

5) Mix all the ingredients in a bowl and set aside.

6) Stir together all the ingredients for the dressing and serve on the side or toss the salad with the dressing, if preferred.

Porcupine Rolls

At the zoo, Barbie and her sisters saw all kinds of awesome animals, big and small. The porcupines gave Chelsea the giggles. But they gave Skipper an idea – for a crafty new recipe.

 ## Ingredients

- 1¼ cups warm water
- 2 tablespoons dry yeast
- ¼ cup honey
- 3½ cups whole wheat flour
- 1 egg
- ⅓ cup vegetable oil
- 1 teaspoon salt
- Sesame seeds and cloves for decorating

. . . .

Instructions

1) Preheat the oven to 400°F.

2) In a bowl, dissolve the yeast in the warm water and add honey.

3) In another bowl, mix together whole wheat flour, the egg, oil, and salt.

4) Mix the ingredients of the two bowls together.

5) Form little balls from the mix and roll one side into sesame seeds.

6) Use cloves for eyes.

7) Bake the porcupine rolls for 10-12 minutes.

Flower Fruits

How does Teresa's garden grow? Splendidly — because it's blooming with colorful flower-fancy treats. It's no surprise Teresa's flowery fruit and vegetable garden is a hit with Barbie and the rest of their friends.

Tomato Tulips

Ingredients

- 10 grape tomatoes
- 1⅔ cups cream cheese
- ¼ cup honey
- 1 teaspoon vanilla extract
- 10 scallions

Instructions

1) Cut an X halfway into the top of each tomato and scoop out the seeds.

2) Put the cream cheese, honey and vanilla in a bowl and whisk together until smooth.

3) Fill the tomatoes with the cream cheese filling.

4) Cut a hole into the bottom of each tomato and put the scallion into that hole for a stem on the "tulip." You can also skip the hole and lay the scallion underneath the "tulip" head for decoration.

Zucchini Daisies

Ingredients

- 1 can tuna packed in water
- ½ small red onion, minced
- ½ cup sour cream
- 2–3 tablespoons mayonnaise
- Pinch sea salt and black pepper
- 1 zucchini
- 2 medium tomatoes

Instructions

1) Make a tuna salad by mixing the tuna, minced onion, sour cream and mayonnaise in a mixing bowl.

2) Add salt and pepper to your taste.

3) Slice the zucchini and tomatoes in thin slices, about a 1/6 inch thick.

4) Put one slice of tomato on top of a slice of zucchini. Add 1–2 tablespoons of the tuna salad and top with a slice of zucchini.

5) Sprinkle sea salt and black pepper in the center of each zucchini top.

Ants on a Log

Ingredients

- 5 celery ribs, ends trimmed
- Cream cheese filling (see tomato tulips)
- Dried cranberries

Instructions

1) Cut the celery sticks in half to make 10 pieces.

2) Spread the same cream cheese filling used in the tomato tulips onto the celery pieces.

3) Sprinkle the cranberries on top.

Caesar Salad

On a trip to the museum, Nikki and Barbie saw priceless treasures from ancient Rome. The giant statue of Caesar was a masterpiece. So was the Caesar salad Nikki served for lunch back home.

 Ingredients

Salad

- 2 heads romaine lettuce
- 4 medium tomatoes
- 1 cup croutons
- 1-2 tablespoons ground black pepper
- ¾ cups parmesan cheese, shaved
- 1½ pounds cooked chicken

Dressing

- 1 cup mayonnaise
- Juice of 1 lemon
- 2 small garlic cloves, crushed
- 1 teaspoon Dijon mustard
- 1 teaspoon Worcestershire sauce
- ½ cup parmesan cheese, grated
- ½ teaspoon sea salt
- ½ teaspoon black pepper

Instructions

1) Mix together all the ingredients for the dressing and set aside.

2) Chop romaine lettuce and tomatoes and mix together in a bowl.

3) Add croutons, pepper and dressing and mix well.

4) If desired, cut the cooked chicken into bite-sized chunks and mix in.

5) Serve on plates or bowls and top with shaved parmesan cheese.

Star Quinoa Salad

Served in a cabbage bowl

Nikki loves salads. So, at Barbie's sleepover party she proudly shared a great new salad she had just discovered: a quinoa salad served inside a bowl that's good enough to eat!

 ## Ingredients

Salad
- 2½ cups white or black quinoa
- 1 small cucumber
- 2 medium tomatoes
- 2 cups arugula
- 1 green apple
- 4 ribs celery
- ½ red onion
- ½ head cabbage

Dressing
- 1 can coconut milk
- Juice of 4 limes
- 1 handful of chopped mint
- 2–3 tablespoons granulated sugar

 ## Instructions

1) Boil the quinoa according to the instructions on the package.

2) Drain and set aside.

3) Chop the cucumber, tomatoes, arugula, apple, celery and red onion into small pieces and mix in a bowl.

4) In a separate bowl, whisk together all the ingredients for the dressing.

5) Add the quinoa and dressing to the diced vegetables and toss together.

6) Serve in a cabbage leaf, like an edible bowl.

Sister Sleepover Pizzas

It's a Sister Sleepover – but who has time to sleep? Especially when Barbie and her sisters have delicious pizzas to bake. For Barbie, Skipper, Stacie, and Chelsea, making pizzas is as easy as pie and super fun, especially when the toppings and dough are as unique as this!

 ## Ingredients

- 2 cups self-rising flour
- 2 teaspoons baking powder
- 1 teaspoon sea salt
- 1½ cups plain yogurt
- ½ cup chopped olives
- 1 tablespoon oregano
- 1 tablespoon thyme
- Goat cheese for topping
- 1 yellow pepper
- Mozzarella cheese for topping
- 2 medium tomatoes, sliced

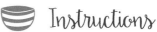 ## Instructions

1) Preheat the oven to 400°F.

2) Mix the flour, baking powder, and sea salt together in a bowl.

3) Divide the dry ingredients evenly between two bowls.

4) Add half of the yogurt into each bowl and knead. Add more flour if the dough is too sticky.

5) Add the chopped olives to one of the bowls and knead into the dough.

6) Add the oregano and thyme to the other bowl of dough.

7) Divide each half of the dough into 5 parts and flatten each part using a rolling pin or just the heel of your hands, making 5 flatbreads, about 1/3 inch thick.

8) Top the olive crusts with the goat cheese and yellow pepper.

9) Top the herb crusts with mozzarella and tomatoes.

10) Bake all of the pizzaz in the oven for 10-15 minutes or until the cheese is completely melted and the crust has turned a golden color.

Cherry Berry Jelly

When the sisters want to have fun, they always come up
with the most juicy ideas. And here is the juiciest idea of all;
a delicious jello recipe with a twist!

Ingredients

- 1 packet cherry flavored gelatin mix
- 2 cups heavy cream
- 2 tablespoons brown sugar
- ½ teaspoon cinnamon
- 4 cinnamon cookies
- 2 cups blackberries
- 4 cherries

Instructions

1) Prepare the jello according to the instructions on the package.

2) Pour the liquid jello evenly into 4 glasses or bowls.

3) Let the jello cool in a refrigerator for 1 hour.

4) Whip the cream until soft peaks form, then add the sugar and cinnamon.

5) Coarsely crumble the cookies.

6) Layer the whipped cream, cookies and blackberries on top of the jello.

7) Add a cherry on top and serve.

Frozen Power Fruit Popsicles

Though Barbie is often busy as a bee, on summer days she loves to boost her energy even further with super-refreshing Frozen Power Fruit Popsicles. These perfect pops are packed with juicy raspberries, apples, blueberries, and coconut.

This recipe requires adult supervision!

Blueberry & Apple

 ### Ingredients

- 3 green apples
- ½ cup water
- ½ cup fresh or frozen raspberries
- ½ cup fresh or frozen blueberries

 ### Instructions

1) Peel and dice the apples.

2) Put the water, apples, and berries into a blender. Place some berries to the side for later.

3) Blend well.

4) Pour into popsicle molds and add extra berries.

5) Freeze overnight or until hardened.

Coco-Berry

 ### Ingredients

- 4 tablespoons honey
- 3 cups coconut water
- Berries and fruit for decoration and flavor

 ### Instructions

1) Mix the honey and coconut water in a blender.

2) Pour the coconut mixture into popsicle molds and add berries, fruit or fresh herbs for decoration and flavor.*

3) Freeze overnight or until hardened.

We used grapes, raspberries, lemon, and fresh mint.

Blueberry
& Apple

Coco-Berry

Green Flower Power

 Ingredients

- 4 green apples
- 1–2 inches fresh ginger
- 1 medium mango

 Instructions

1) Peel and chop the apples, ginger and mango.

2) Put all the ingredients into a blender, except for a few mango slices.

3) Blend well.

4) Pour into popsicle molds and add extra mango slices.

5) Freeze overnight or until hardened.

Mango-Berry

Ingredients

- 1 pineapple
- 2 medium mangoes
- ½ cup fresh or frozen raspberries

Instructions

1) Peel and chop the pineapple and mangoes. This can be a bit tricky, so ask for help from an adult.

2) Put the chopped pineapple and mango into a blender until the fruit is well blended.

3) Pour into popsicle molds and add raspberries.

4) Freeze overnight or until hardened.

Mango-Berry &
Green Flower Power

Ice Crush

What's cooler for Barbie than going on a hike with her sisters? Enjoying a tall glass of frosty, flavorful ice afterwards, of course! Packed with tasty fruit and zesty mint, these icy drinks are cool fuel.

Pineapple – Apple

- ½ fresh pineapple
- 2 cups fresh apple juice

1) Peel and cut the pineapple. This can be a bit tricky so ask an adult to help you.

2) Put all ingredients in a blender and blend thoroughly.

3) Place the juice in the freezer for at least 4 hours or overnight.

4) To serve, scrape the frozen juice with a fork to make fluffy, coarse snow.

Lime

- ½ avocado
- 2½ cups fresh apple juice
- 4 limes
- Zest from 2 limes

1) Peel the avocado.

2) Place the avocado, apple juice and lemon zest in a blender. Squeeze the juice from the limes over the mix and blend well.

3) Put the juice in the freezer for at least 4 hours or overnight.

4) To serve, scrape the frozen juice with a fork to make fluffy, coarse snow.

Blueberry – Apple

- 2½ cups fresh apple juice
- 1 cup blueberries

1) Put the blueberries in a blender, pour the apple juice over and blend well.

2) Place the juice in the freezer for at least 4 hours or overnight.

3) To serve, scrape the frozen juice with a fork to make fluffy, coarse snow.

Watermelon – Mint

- 2 pounds seedless watermelon
- 2 limes
- 1 handful of fresh mint

1) Cut up the watermelon.

2) Put the watermelon and mint in a blender and squeeze the juice from the limes over it.

3) Blend thoroughly.

4) Place the juice in the freezer for at least 4 hours or overnight.

5) To serve, scrape the frozen juice with a fork to make fluffy, coarse snow.

Dinner

Spaghetti & Meatballs

Wherever Skipper goes, so does her phone! How can her sisters get Skipper's attention for just a few minutes? Bring on Skipper's favorite meal of spaghetti and meatballs. Not only is it delish, but those strands of spaghetti are seriously fun to eat, too. Who needs to text when you can twirl?

This recipe requires adult supervision!

 ## Ingredients

Meatballs
- 1 pound ground beef
- 16 saltine crackers
- 1 tablespoon fresh parsley
- 1 tablespoon fresh basil
- 1 egg
- ¼ cup parmesan cheese
- ½ teaspoon sea salt
- ½ teaspoon ground black pepper

Tomato sauce
- ½ cup sundried tomatoes
- 1 small tomato
- ½ cup olive oil
  - Juice from 1 lemon
  - 1 handful of fresh basil
  - 1 teaspoon oregano
  - Pinch of red chili flakes
  - 1½ teaspoons salt
  - 1 small red bell pepper

- 7 oz spaghetti
- 1 teaspoon sea salt

Instructions

1) Preheat the oven to 400°F.

2) Put the beef in a large bowl.

3) Crush the crackers and add to the bowl.

4) Finely chop the fresh basil and parsley and add to the beef.

5) Add all other meatball ingredients to the beef and mix well with your hands.

6) With wet hands, form the beet mixture into balls. You can make any size you'd like, but meatballs are usually the size of a golf ball.

7) Place the meatballs in a pan or on a baking sheet and cook in the oven for 15-20 minutes. The bigger the meatballs are, the longer they need in the oven.

8) Bring water to a boil in a saucepan and add salt.

9) Add the spaghetti to the boiling water and cook according to the instructions on the package.

10) Put all the ingredients for the sauce into a food processor or blender and mix well.

11) Heat the sauce in a saucepan over medium heat until it is warm.

12) Put the cooked pasta on a big serving plate and arrange the meatballs on top.

13) Pour the tomato sauce over the spaghetti and meatballs and serve.

Chicken Skewers

School, friends, skateboarding, surfboarding – Stacie's schedule is as extreme as her sports. So when she works up an appetite, the first thing she craves is her superlicious chicken skewers. This dish is not just yummy, it's also easy to make.

This recipe requires adult supervision!

 ## Ingredients

- *2 inch piece of fresh ginger, minced*
- *2 garlic cloves, minced*
- *½ red chili, minced*
- *2 tablespoons maple syrup*
- *1-2 tablespoons tamari or soy sauce*
- *¼ cup lemon juice*
- *½ cup peanut butter*
- *1 lb boneless skinless chicken*

. . . .

Instructions

1) Preheat the oven to 350°F.

2) In a blender, mix the first 6 ingredients well.

3) Add the peanut butter and blend.

4) Split the sauce you have made into two small bowls.

5) Cut the chicken into thin strips and brush with one half of the sauce.

6) Thread the chicken onto skewers and place on a greased baking sheet.

7) Bake for 15–20 minutes, or until fully cooked. That means that there is no pink anywhere on the chicken.

8) Serve with the other half of the sauce.

Chicken Wraps

What's worse for Skipper than a low wi-fi signal? Low energy! So when Skipper needs a pick-me-up, she cooks up a meal of her favorite yummy chicken wraps. Not only is this energy-packed dish fun to make, it's fun to share with friends — or three hungry sisters!

 ## Ingredients

Peanut sauce

- 1 teaspoon ground ginger
- Juice of 2 lemons
- 2 tablespoons soy sauce
- 2 tablespoons apple cider vinegar
- ⅓ cup maple syrup
- ½ cup peanut butter

Chicken Wraps

- 1½ pounds cooked chicken breast
- Salt & pepper
- 1 red onion
- 3 bell peppers
- 4 handfuls of spinach
- 4 tortillas

Instructions

1) Put all the ingredients for the sauce, except for the peanut butter, in a bowl and mix well.

2) Add ½ cup of peanut butter, or more if you want a thicker sauce.

3) Cut the chicken breast into thin strips and add salt and pepper.

4) Cut the onion and bell peppers into strips.

5) Put a handful of spinach leaves on each tortilla. Add ¼ of the chicken and vegetables and roll tightly.

6) Serve with the peanut sauce for dipping.

Fantastic Sliders & Fries

Barbie loves learning new things and she loves surprising her friends. So when she learns how to make delicious mini-burgers, she invites everyone over for an impromptu barbeque!

Ingredients

Fries
- 2 small sweet potatoes
- 3 tablespoons olive oil
- 1 teaspoon sea salt

Sliders
- 5 medium-sized mushrooms
- 2 tablespoons tamari or soy sauce
- 20 mini hamburger buns or 5 large hamburger buns, quartered
- 4 tablespoons of your favorite sauce
- 10 spinach leaves
- 14 oz cooked beef or lamb fillet
- Salt and pepper to taste

Instructions

1) Preheat the oven to 450°F.

2) Cut the sweet potatoes into strips.

3) Roll the strips of potatoes in 1 tablespoon olive oil and salt, to taste.

4) Place the sweet potato strips on an baking tray. Make sure that the strips are not placed too close together so that they do not touch. Bake for 20-30 minutes (depending on size), turning them occasionally.

5) While the potatoes bake in the oven, slice the mushrooms and fry them in 2 tablespoons olive oil and the tamari or soy sauce for 4-5 minutes and set them aside.

Assembly

1) Cut the hamburger buns in half.

2) Put a small amount of your chosen sauce on each half.

3) On the bottom half of the hamburger bun, place a leaf of spinach, followed by a slice of the cooked fillet and, finally, a slice of the fried mushrooms.

4) Put the other half of the hamburger bun on top and place a skewer through the middle.

Three Cheese Lasagna

Teresa's grandma has decided to share her super-secret lasagna recipe. Teresa can't wait to make it! And when Teresa cooks the dish for Barbie and Nikki, it'll be no secret it's delicious!

Ingredients

Tomato sauce
- 2 tablespoons olive oil
- 4 garlic cloves, minced
- 2 scallions, chopped
- 1 can diced tomatoes
- 2 tablespoons fresh basil, chopped
- Salt and pepper

Cheese filling
- 2 cups cottage cheese
- ½ cup grated mozzarella cheese
- 1 egg white
- 2 tablespoons olive oil
- 2 tablespoons fresh flat-leaf parsley, chopped
- ½ teaspoon sea salt

Lasagna
- ½ cup grated mozzarella
- ½ cup grated Parmesan cheese
- 15 lasagna sheets

Instructions

Tomato sauce
1) In a saucepan, heat the olive oil over medium-high heat.

2) Add the garlic and whisk until fragrant, about 2 minutes.

3) Add the chopped scallions and continue to whisk for 1-2 minutes.

4) Add diced tomatoes and bring to a boil. Lower the heat and let simmer for about 20 minutes.

5) Remove from the heat and add fresh basil and salt and pepper to taste.

6) Set aside.

Cheese filling
1) In a large bowl, beat together the cottage cheese, mozzarella cheese, and egg white, and set aside.

2) In a saucepan, heat 2 tablespoons of olive oil over medium heat.

3) Add the chopped parsley to the cheese bowl and blend well.

Lasagna
1) Preheat the oven to 375°F.

2) Lightly coat a 9-by-13-inch baking dish with cooking spray.

3) Spread ⅓ of the tomato sauce in the dish and cover with 3 sheets of the pasta.

4) Add ½ of the cheese mixture onto the pasta and spread gently.

5) Cover with 3 more pasta sheets.

6) Repeat until you have finished all the sauce and then add another 3 pasta sheets.

7) Top the lasagna with ½ cup grated mozzarella cheese and ½ cup grated parmesan cheese.

8) Cover loosely with foil and bake for 25 minutes.

9) Remove the foil and bake until golden, about 10 minutes.

10) Let stand for 10 minutes before serving.

11) Serve with chopped fresh vegetables or bread.

Quesadilla

This recipe requires adult supervision!

A quesadilla is perfect for a party, but Nikki's recipe needed more pizzazz. So she and Barbie got together to swap ideas. Soon there was more than just ideas flying around, but tortillas, corn, and colorful peppers, as she and Barbie got creative in the kitchen. The result was a quesadilla fit for a fiesta!

Ingredients

- 1 can refried beans
- 8 tortillas
- 2 tomatoes
- 3 bell peppers
- 1 can corn, drained
- 2 cups grated mozzarella cheese

Instructions

1) Preheat oven to 400°F.

2) Spread refried beans on four tortillas.

3) Finely chop the tomatoes and bell peppers.

4) Divide the corn between the four tortillas.

5) Add a quarter of the chopped peppers and tomatoes to each tortilla.

6) Sprinkle a quarter of the grated cheese on top of each of the four tortillas.

7) Top each of the quesadillas with another tortilla. This will leave you with four tortilla "sandwiches."

8) Bake in the oven for 6-8 minutes and serve with fresh cilantro, guacamole and sour cream.

Stuffed Sweet Potatoes

Who says stuffing has to be reserved for turkeys? Barbie's baked sweet potatoes are stuffed with corn, cheese, guacamole and sour cream.

 Ingredients

Sweet potatoes

- 4 sweet potatoes
- 1 small can kidney beans
- 1 small can yellow corn
- 2 sprigs scallions
- 1 small tomato
- ½ red pepper
- ½ green pepper

Guacamole

- 1 avocado
- Juice from ½ lemon
- 1 tablespoon minced red onion
- 2 tablespoons finely chopped tomato
- 1 tablespoon finely chopped fresh cilantro
- Pinch sea salt
- Pinch dry chili flakes

 Instructions

Sweet potatoes

1) Preheat oven to 400°F.

2) Pierce the potatoes a few times with a fork and bake them for 45 minutes to an hour, depending on size.

3) Drain and rinse the kidney beans and yellow corn and combine in a bowl.

4) Chop the scallions and tomato and add to the bowl.

5) Dice the red and green peppers and add to the bowl and mix all the ingredients.

6) Remove the potatoes from the oven and let them cool a bit before you cut them open across the top and stuff with the mix.

7) Serve with sour cream and guacamole.

Guacamole
Mix all ingredients into a creamy dip.

Noodle Salad

With honey-chili dressing

Teresa is one of the best cooks Barbie knows. But can she win first prize at the school's cooking contest? No problem! With her tasty noodles, Teresa totally wows the judges – and wins the contest!

 ## Ingredients

- 2 tablespoons vegetable oil
- 2 bunches broccolini
- 6 oz noodles
- 2 handfuls of arugula (or spinach)
- 2 slices fresh pineapple
- 2 carrots
- Handful of fresh cilantro
- Handful of fresh mint

Honey-chili dressing

- ½ teaspoon red chili paste
- 1 cup fresh orange juice
- ⅓ cup honey
- ½ cup extra virgin olive oil

 ## Instructions

1) Heat the vegetable oil in a pan over medium heat.

2) Trim about 1½ inches off the broccolini stems and discard.

3) Slice the broccolini in half lengthwise and sauté on the pan for 1-2 minutes. Set aside.

4) Cook the noodles according to the instructions on the package. Set aside.

5) Chop the arugula coarsely.

6) Cut the pineapple and carrots into small pieces.

7) Mix the broccolini and chopped vegetables, fruit, and herbs with the noodles.

8) Add the honey-chili dressing and serve.

Honey-chili dressing

1) Blend chili paste, orange juice, and honey in a blender.

2) Keep the blender running on high speed while slowly adding the olive oil. This will make the dressing creamy and thick.

Sweets

Chocolate Cupcakes

Skipper and her friends won the most amazing contest. Not only will they see their favorite band perform, they'll get to meet them backstage! The band is lucky, too. Skipper is bringing her famous chocolate cupcakes to share!

 Ingredients

Cupcakes

- 3 large eggs
- 1½ cups granulated sugar
- ¾ cup butter, at room temperature
- 1½ cups dark chocolate chips
- ½ cup milk
- 1½ cups all-purpose flour
- 2 teaspoons baking powder

Frosting

- ⅔ cup butter, at room temperature
- ¾ cup icing sugar
- ¾ cup cocoa
- 1 tablespoon vanilla sugar
- 4 tablespoons syrup

Instructions

Cupcakes

1) Preheat the oven to 380°F.

2) Whisk the eggs and sugar until light and golden.

3) Melt the butter and chocolate together in a saucepan over low heat. You can also melt this in the microwave.

4) Add the milk.

5) Add the butter, milk, and chocolate to the egg mixture.

6) Fold in the flour and baking powder.

7) Distribute evenly in 20 cupcake molds bake on the middle rack of the oven for about 15 minutes.

Frosting

1) Beat the butter, cocoa, and icing sugar together.

2) Beat in the vanilla sugar and syrup.

White Chocolate Mousse

Who doesn't love fun surprises, especially when they are as delicious as this one? One day Barbie wanted to surprise her friend Teresa with the most awesome sweet treat. But when a simple chocolate mousse won't cut it, what's a girl to do? Answer: kick it up a notch with some juicy ripe strawberries and crunchy ginger crust!

 ## Ingredients

White chocolate mousse
- 1 gelatin sheet
- Water to dissolve the gelatin
- 12 ounces white chocolate
- 2 cups cream

Crust
- 3 graham crackers
- 1 tablespoon brown sugar

Strawberry sauce
- 1 cup strawberries
- 1 tablespoon maple syrup

Instructions

1) Dissolve the gelatin in water.

2) Melt the white chocolate in a saucepan over very low heat.

3) Add the cream slowly to the melted chocolate. Keep stirring while you pour the cream.

4) Add the gelatin mixture into the chocolate and cream and stir.

5) Put the chocolate blend in the refrigerator and let sit for 2-3 hours.

6) In a blender, mix together half of the strawberries and all the maple syrup and set aside.

7) Dice the remaining strawberries.

8) Crush the graham crackers and mix them with the brown sugar. Set aside.

9) Find a big mason jar or a tall glass and put half of the crust in the bottom of the glass.

10) Add a layer of the diced strawberries on top of the crust.

11) Add a layer of the mousse, followed by a second layer of crust. Keep a small amount of crust aside for the top of the dessert.

12) Add the strawberry sauce on top of the crust and the rest of the mousse on top of the sauce.

13) Finish off by sprinkling the rest of the crust on top and use a strawberry as a garnish.

Flower Cake

With choco-meringue

Always texting and gaming, Skipper is a gadget girl and proud of it. Now Skipper has a new gadget to add to her supply: a kitchen whisk. She also has a sweet new recipe to try it out on, for light-as-a-petal Flower Cake!

Ingredients

Bottom layer:
Chocolate cake
- 2 eggs
- 1 cup granulated sugar
- ¾ cups dark chocolate chips
- ⅔ cups butter
- 1 cup all-purpose flour
- 1 teaspoon baking powder

Middle layer:
Meringue
- 2 egg whites
- ½ cup caster sugar

Top layer:
Whipped cream
- 2 cups heavy cream
- 1 cup blueberries
- 1 cup strawberries, cut in half

Instructions

Bottom layer
1) Preheat oven to 310°F.

2) Melt the butter and chocolate together in a saucepan over low heat or in the microwave.

3) Whisk the eggs and sugar until light and golden.

4) Add the melted chocolate and butter and mix well.

5) Carefully fold in the all-purpose flour and baking powder.

6) Pour into two 9 inch, round forms and bake for 30–35 minutes.

Middle layer
1) Preheat oven to 210°F.

2) Whisk the egg whites until stiff peaks form.

3) Add the sugar slowly and keep whisking.

4) Line a baking sheet with parchment paper.

5) Draw a 9-inch circle on the parchment paper.

6) Spread the mixture evenly into the circle and bake for 1 hour.

7) Leave the oven door closed to prevent the meringue from cracking and let the meringue cool.

Assembly
1) Place a meringue circle on top of the chocolate cake.

2) Whip the heavy cream to soft peaks and put on top of the meringue.

3) Cut the strawberries in half and place them on top of the cream.

4) Decorate the cake with blueberries and put beautiful flowers on top (only for decoration).

Raspberry Lemon Ice Cream

When life throws Barbie lemons, she fills them with ice cream, sugar, raspberries, and other delectable eats. Then she has a garden party to share them with her best friends. This lemony dessert is super sweet!

 ## Ingredients

- 3 eggs
- 3 lemons
- ⅔ cups granulated sugar
- 1 cup mascarpone cheese
- ½ cup raspberries
- 1 cup heavy whipping cream

Instructions

1) Separate the egg yolks from the egg whites.

2) Whisk the egg yolks and sugar together until small foam begins to appear.

3) Add the mascarpone and then the raspberries and mix well.

4) In another bowl, whisk the heavy cream until stiff peaks form.

5) In a third bowl, whisk the egg whites until stiff peaks form.

6) Carefully fold the ingredients of the 3 bowls together to make ice cream.

7) Cut the top 1/4 off the lemons. Using a metal spoon, scoop out their insides, leaving just the outer shell.

8) Place the ice cream in the hollowed out lemons and put in the freezer for 2 hours or over night.

9) Just before serving, decorate each lemon with chopped raspberries.

Blueberry Muffins

Nikki and Barbie love teaching each other new things.
So when Nikki told Barbie about her recipe for blueberry muffins
with a tasty twist, Barbie knew she had to learn it!

 ## Ingredients

Makes about 12 muffins

- 1 cup all-purpose flour
- 1 cup whole wheat flour
- 1 teaspoon baking powder
- 1 teaspoon baking soda
- Pinch sea salt
- ½ cup brown sugar
- 1 egg
- ⅓ cup olive oil
- 1 cup yogurt
- 1 cup blueberries (fresh or frozen)
- ½ cup chocolate chips

 ## Instructions

1) Preheat the oven to 350°F.

2) Blend the all-purpose and whole wheat flour, baking powder, baking soda, salt and brown sugar in a bowl.

3) In a separate bowl, whisk the eggs and add the olive oil and yogurt.

4) Add the dry ingredients into the egg mixture.

5) Stir in the blueberries and chocolate chips.

6) Bake in muffin forms for about 25 minutes and let cool for a while before serving.

Banana Blasts

Cinnamon spiced, chocolate covered bananas

Stacie is always on the move, until a sudden craving stops her in her tracks. That's when she goes bananas in the kitchen, topping her favorite fruit with cinnamon, sprinkles and melted chocolate. Like Stacie's sports, this snack is extreme ... extremely bananalicious!

 ## Ingredients

- *4 bananas*
- *2 teaspoons cinnamon*
- *1½ cups chocolate chips*
- *Colored sprinkles for decoration*

Instructions

1) Peel the bananas and cut each one in two halves.

2) Dust the bananas with cinnamon.

3) Melt the chocolate in a pan over very low heat (or in a microwave).

4) Put a stick into each banana half and dip the banana in the melted chocolate to coat.

5) Dip the chocolate covered banana into sprinkles and then let it dry in a cooler before serving.

Very Berry Birthday Cake

Teresa sure knows how to enjoy the best things in life. When she wants to share the joy with Barbie, she makes this savory and sweet, very berry birthday cake. Now every day can feel like someone's birthday!

 ## Ingredients

- 3 eggs
- 1½ cups granulated sugar
- ¾ cups butter
- ¾ cups dark chocolate chips
- 1½ cups all-purpose flour
- 1½ teaspoons baking powder
- 15 large strawberries

Frosting
- ½ cup butter, at room temperature
- 3 cups icing sugar
- 1–2 teaspoons vanilla extract
- 1–2 tablespoons milk

Instructions

1) Preheat the oven to 310°F.

2) Thoroughly whisk together the eggs and sugar.

3) Melt the butter and dark chocolate together in a saucepan over low heat or in a microwave.

4) Add the chocolate mixture to the eggs.

5) Carefully fold in the flour and baking powder.

6) Pour the cake batter into two round 9 inch cake forms and bake for 30-35 minutes.

7) To make the frosting, whisk together the butter, icing sugar and vanilla extract until smooth.

8) Add milk to the frosting to achieve your desired consistency. However, if you like the texture and taste of the frosting without the milk you can skip this step.

9) Remove the cakes from the oven and let them cool completely.

10) Frost one cake with half the frosting and then top with the second cake.

11) Spread the rest of the frosting on top of the cake.

12) Cut the tops off the strawberries and arrange them, bottoms up, on top of the cake before serving.

Friendship Treats

Barbie loves to celebrate, whether it's a birthday, the holidays or herself for acing a pop quiz.But one day Barbie took celebrating to a whole new level. She celebrated her best friends with a toasty batch of sprinkled peanut butter Friendship Treats. And, even better, she served them with a tasty side of sweet strawberry milk!

This recipe requires adult supervision!

Ingredients

Friendship Treats
- 8 slices wholegrain bread
- Peanut butter
- Blueberry jelly
- Colored sprinkles

Sweet Strawberry milk
- ¼ cup hot water from the kettle
- 1 pound strawberries, cleaned and chopped
- ¾ cup granulated sugar
- 1 teaspoon vanilla extract
- Milk

Instructions

Sweet slices

1) Toast the bread lightly.

2) Spread peanut butter and blueberry jelly on each slice of toasted bread.

3) Stack four pieces of bread to make a sandwich.

4) Cut the sandwich diagonally across, into 4 triangles.

5) Dip one side of each triangle into the colored sprinkles.

Sweet Strawberry milk

1) Heat the water in a kettle.

2) Put the strawberries, sugar, and vanilla extract in a blender and mix on medium speed.

3) Strain the strawberry mixture through a fine mesh sieve or a paper coffee filter, trying to extract as much syrup as possible into a small bowl.

4) Put in the refrigerator and let cool completely.

5) To serve, mix 1 part strawberry with 4 parts milk and enjoy!

Quirky Dirt Dessert

Chelsea loves throwing parties about as much as her friends love going to them! What makes Chelsea's parties extra sweet? Her deliciously quirky dirt dessert, that's what. "Dirty" gummy worms, anyone?

This recipe requires adult supervision!

 Ingredients

- 2 bananas
- 1 avocado
- ½ cup unsweetened cocoa powder
- 4 tablespoons honey
- 8 dark chocolate cookies
- Gummy worms

Instructions

1) Put the chocolate cookies into a sealable plastic bag and crush them to make a cookie crumble. Set aside.

2) Blend the bananas and avocado in a food processor until smooth.

3) Add the unsweetened cocoa powder to the banana mix and blend well to make chocolate pudding.

4) Sweeten with honey to your desired taste.

5) Put some of the cookie crumble in the bottom of a Mason jar or serving bowl.

6) Spoon chocolate pudding on top of the cookie crumble base and then sprinkle with more cookie crumbles.

7) Decorate with gummy worms.

Chocolate Truffles

Stacie's soccer team played an awesome game. Now they have a new goal: to team up and make the most awesome snacks ever – these coconutty chocolate truffles.

Ingredients

- ⅓ cup coconut oil or very soft butter
- ⅓ cup maple syrup
- 1 teaspoon vanilla extract
- ⅛ teaspoon sea salt
- ½ cup shredded coconut
- 1¼ cup cocoa powder

Instructions

1) If you are using coconut oil, place the closed jar in warm water until the oil is melted. If you are using butter, make sure that is very soft so it can easily be mixed with the other ingredients.

2) In a bowl, thoroughly mix together the coconut oil (or butter), maple syrup, vanilla extract, salt and shredded coconut.

3) Add 1 cup of cocoa powder to the bowl and mix well.

4) Place the bowl in the refrigerator for 30 minutes.

5) Once well chilled, use a spoon or melon baller to scoop small amounts of the chocolate mixture and roll it between your hands to form 1 inch balls.

6) Roll each ball in the remaining ¼ cup cocoa powder to coat.

7) You can also roll the balls in the shredded coconut.

8) Store in the refrigerator until ready to serve!

Mini Cupcakes with Raspberries

Little sister Chelsea knows that good things come in small packages. When she needed a gift for her teacher, Chelsea knew just what to make! Chelsea and Barbie baked the yummiest batch of mini cupcakes with raspberries.

 Ingredients

- *1 cup butter*
- *5 eggs*
- *2 cups icing sugar*
- *2 cups all-purpose flour*
- *1 cup raspberries (fresh or frozen)*

 Instructions

1) Preheat oven to 400°F.

2) Melt the butter in a saucepan over medium heat.

3) Lightly whisk the eggs.

4) Add the melted butter, icing sugar and flour to the eggs and combine well.

5) Spoon the batter into a cupcake tin, filling each mold ¾ full.

6) Add 2-3 raspberries to the top of each cupcake and place the tin in the oven.

7) Bake for about 15 minutes, for mini cupcakes, or 25 minutes for larger ones.

8) Let the cupcakes cool completely and then remove from the cupcake tin. Dust with icing sugar before serving.

Barbie's No-Bake Cake

For Chelsea, there's just one thing more fun than helping Barbie prepare her yummy-for-the-tummy white chocolate cake — helping Barbie, Skipper, and Stacie eat it!

 Ingredients

- 2¼ cups white chocolate chips
- ⅓ cup olive oil
- 3 packs wafers, vanilla and/or chocolate
- 1 box red grapes
- Icing sugar for decoration

 Instructions

1) Melt the white chocolate in a saucepan over medium heat.

2) Add olive oil to the melted chocolate and mix well.

3) Pour a thin layer of the melted chocolate mixture into a bread pan, just enough to cover the bottom.

4) Layer the wafers in the bread pan. If using vanilla and chocolate wafers, alternate between the two flavors for each layer. Make sure that there is space between the wafers and the sides of the bread pan.

5) Pour the remaining chocolate mixture over the wafers to cover and fill the gaps between the wafers and the sides of the bread pan.

6) Let cool in a refrigerator until the chocolate has set.

7) Invert to remove the cake from the bread pan. Decorate with grapes and dust with icing sugar.

Index

Oil & liquids

Apple juice	46
Apple cider vinegar	54
Coconut water	42
Coconut oil	86
Extra virgin olive oil	12, 28, 64
Honey	12, 20, 30, 32, 42, 64, 84
Lemon juice	34, 50, 52, 54, 62
Maple Syrup	14, 20, 52, 54, 70, 86
Olive oil	18, 50, 54, 56, 58, 76, 90
Orange juice	64
Peanut butter	20, 54, 82
Soy sauce	52, 54
Syrup	68
Tamari sauce	52
Vanilla extract	20, 32, 80, 82
Vegetable oil	16, 22, 64
Water	30, 34, 42, 70, 82

Noodles, pasta & rice

Lasagna sheets	58
Noodles	64
Spaghetti	50

Sauces & other

Blueberry jelly	82
Chocolate chips	76, 78
Cinnamon cookies	40
Dark chocolate	68, 72, 80
Dark chocolate cookies	84
Gelatin sheet	70
Graham crackers	70
Gummy worms	84
Mayonnaise	32, 34
Salty crackers	50
Spicy mustard	364
Sprinkles	78, 82
Tomato salsa	22
Wafers	90
Worchestershire sauce	34
White chocolate	70, 90
Yeast	30

Spices

Basil	50, 58
Chili flakes	50, 62, 64
Cilantro	62, 64
Cinnamon	14, 20, 40, 78
Flat-leaf parsley	58
Mint	64
Oregano	38, 50
Parsley	50
Pepper	28, 32, 34, 50, 54, 56, 58
Red pepper flakes	16
Salt	10, 12, 16, 18, 20, 26, 28, 30, 32, 34, 38, 50, 54, 56, 58, 62, 76, 86
Thyme	38
Vanilla	86
White pepper	18

Vegetables & beans

Arugula	36, 64
Bell pepper	16, 18, 22, 38, 54, 62
Black beans	62
Broccolini	64
Cabbage	36
Carrots	22, 64
Celery	32, 36
Chili	52
Cilantro, fresh	22, 28
Cucumber	36
Garlic cloves	34, 52, 58
Ginger	44, 52, 54
Mint leaves, fresh	28
Olives	38
Pomegranate	28
Red onion	28, 32, 36, 54, 62
Refried beans	60
Romaine lettuce	28, 34
Scallions	32, 58, 62
Spinach	16, 44, 54, 64
Sweet corn	60, 62
Sweet potatoes	56, 62
Sun-dried tomatoes	50
Tomatoes	32, 34, 36, 38, 50, 60, 62
Tomatoes, crushed	58
Zucchini	32

Recipes in alphabetical order